Night
Animals

Susan Meredith
Designed by Nicola Butler
and Josephine Thompson

Illustrated by Patrizia Donaera
and Adam Larkum

Night animals consultant: Margaret Rostron
Reading consultant: Alison Kelly, Roehampton University

This is a photo of a flying squirrel.

Contents

Busy at night

Thousands of animals are out and about at night. They are called nocturnal animals.

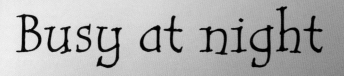

Raccoons are nocturnal. They stay wide-awake all night.

Night feasts

Night animals eat in the dark. Some find more food at night. Others feel safer then.

A leopard waits for an animal to pass by.

It leaps down and kills it with a bite.

It drags it up into a tree to eat it.

Night monkeys eat fruit. They grab their share while other monkeys are asleep.

Big birds can attack koalas. Koalas munch leaves at night, while the birds are asleep.

Bushbabies

Bushbabies are night animals that live in trees.

They run and jump from branch to branch at night.

A bushbaby moves its ears to tell where sounds come from.

If it hears an insect, it grabs it out of the air and eats it.

6

A mother bushbaby carries her baby around in her mouth.

She leaves it clinging to a twig while she goes to look for food.

A bushbaby's long tail helps it balance in the air.

Bushbabies comb their fur with one long claw.

Big eyes

Lots of night animals have big bulgy eyes. This helps them to see in the dark.

Tarsiers have the biggest eyes of any animal their size.

This tarsier has caught a huge insect to eat but it can spot tiny ones too.

Geckos open their eyes
wide to see in the dark.

Light hurts a night animal's eyes. The black
part shrinks in the day to keep light out.

Some frogs' eyes
narrow to a thin
slit in daylight.

The black part
of a tiger's eyes
shrinks to a dot.

Geckos peer out
from four tiny
holes in a slit.

Listen and sniff

It isn't always easy to see in the dark. Night animals need to smell and hear well too.

Aardvarks have long ears and long snouts.

They listen for ants and sniff out their nests.

Aardvarks dig up ants' nests with their claws.

They trap the ants on their sticky tongue.

Gila monsters sniff and lick the ground to tell if there is food around.

Fennec foxes are the smallest foxes in the world but they have the biggest ears.

They can hear mice, lizards and even insects from a long way off.

11

Owls

Owls are lucky birds. They find lots to eat but nothing wants to eat them.

An owl has big wings. It doesn't need to flap them a lot.

Its feathers are soft and fluffy. They don't make a noise.

Other animals don't hear the owl coming and get pounced on.

Owls can't move their eyes but can turn their heads almost all the way around to look at things.

Owls can see and hear very well. This owl's ears are not where you might expect.

Feathers

Ear

Too hot

Some animals can't stand the heat of the sun and come out at night when it is cooler.

At night, hippos feed on grass.

In the day they sit in water to cool off. They cover themselves with mud like a sunblock.

Slugs come out at night because they would dry up and die in the sun.

Kangaroo rats live in hot deserts. They dig
burrows under the sand with their feet.
It is cooler underground.

At night
the rats hop
around like
kangaroos.

They pick up
seeds and
stuff them in
their mouths.

They empty
them in their
burrows to
eat next day.

Daytime sleep

Most night animals stay in their home during the day and go to sleep.

Dormice make nests of hay to sleep in.

Nut to eat

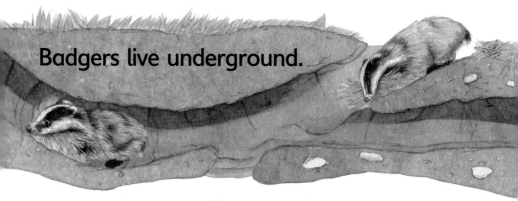

Badgers live underground.

They carry their bedding under their chin and sometimes bring it up to air in the sun.

Sloths spend their lives
hanging upside down in trees.
They even sleep this way.

Sloths move around
so little that plants
grow in their hair.

17

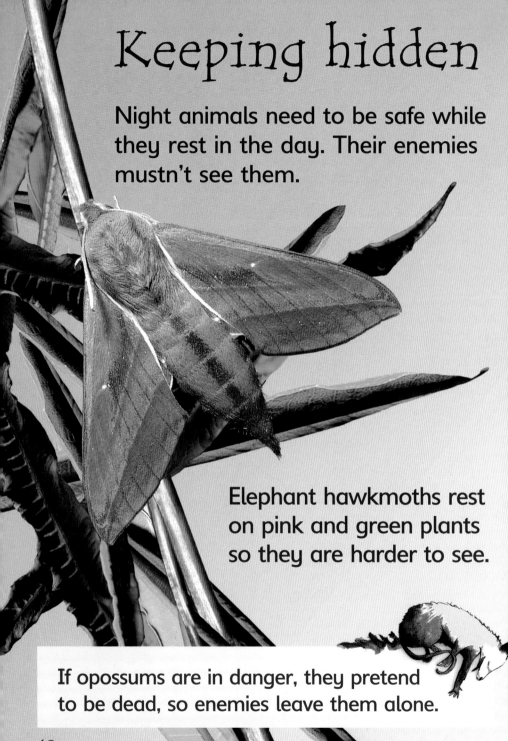

Keeping hidden

Night animals need to be safe while they rest in the day. Their enemies mustn't see them.

Elephant hawkmoths rest on pink and green plants so they are harder to see.

If opossums are in danger, they pretend to be dead, so enemies leave them alone.

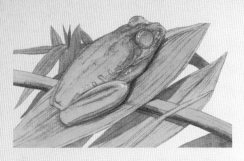 

Red-eyed tree frogs hide on leaves in the daytime, like this.

If they get woken up, their bright eyes and legs scare off enemies.

This bird is a frogmouth. The marks on its feathers make it look like a branch.

Bats

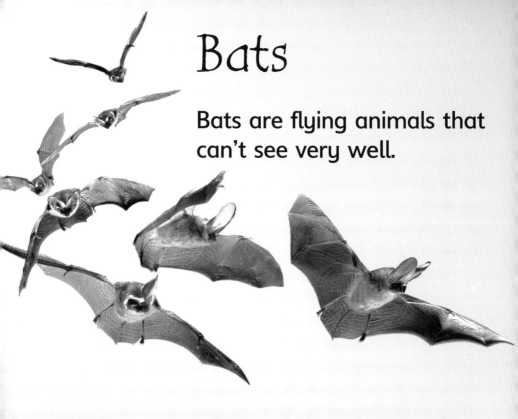

Bats are flying animals that can't see very well.

Some bats eat insects. They find them by using their ears in a strange way.

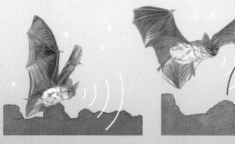

A bat makes lots of high squeaks as it flies along.

The squeaks hit an insect and bounce back off it.

The bat hears the squeaks. It scoops up the insect.

Fruit bats can smell ripe
fruit from far away.

They eat it hanging upside down.

Some bats eat fish, which they grab
out of the water with their claws.

Night noises

While people are fast asleep, animals call to each other in the dark.

Wolves can recognize each other's voices.

They howl to other wolves in their pack, and to tell outsiders to keep away.

Night monkey families don't
like other families to come too close.
They chatter at them until they go away.

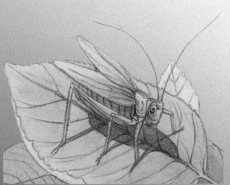

A male cricket chirps
a song by rubbing
his wings together.

A female likes the
song and comes to
find the male.

Light messages

Some night animals have strange ways of sending messages.

Fireflies flash like lights to send signals to one another. This tree is full of fireflies.

A firefly makes a flash with its tummy.

Frogs eat fireflies. If they eat too many, they glow.

Black dragonfish have a
light dangling from their
chin. Shrimps come to
look at it and are eaten.

Female glow-worms
can make their bodies
glow with light.

Male glow-worms
fly to meet the
glowing females.

Hedgehogs

Hedgehogs hunt for food at night when there are insects, worms and slugs around.

A hedgehog sniffs out worms, then digs them up.

If a fox comes, the hedgehog rolls itself into a prickly ball.

The fox is hungry but doesn't like prickles, so it goes away.

These baby hedgehogs are only a few days old.

They haven't opened their eyes yet and their prickles are not too sharp.

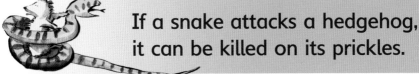

If a snake attacks a hedgehog, it can be killed on its prickles.

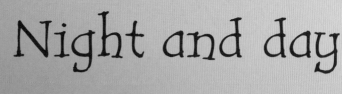

Night and day

Some animals are out and about in the day as well as at night.

Tigers and other big cats hunt mainly at night. Smaller cats like to do the same.

A cat's eyes shine brightly in the dark.

Kangaroos are mostly night animals although they sunbathe in the daytime.

Rabbits get too hot in the day and too cold at night.

They come out just as it is getting dark or getting light.

Foxes used to come out only at night to find other animals to eat.

Now, they come out in the day too, to eat food scraps that people leave lying around.

Glossary

Here are some of the words in this book you might not know. This page tells you what they mean.

 nocturnal - awake and busy at night. Nocturnal animals rest during the day.

 hunt - to look for, catch and kill animals, usually to eat.

 snout - the long nose and mouth parts of an animal's face.

 claw - the hard, sharp, curved parts at the end of animals' fingers or toes.

 burrow - a hole or tunnel that an animal digs in the ground to live in.

 male - an animal that can become a father. Boys and men are male.

 female - an animal that can become a mother. Girls and women are female.

Websites to visit

You can visit exciting websites to find out more about night animals.

To visit these websites, go to the Usborne Quicklinks Website at **www.usborne-quicklinks.com** Read the internet safety guidelines, and then type the keywords **"beginners night animals"**.

The websites are regularly reviewed and the links in Usborne Quicklinks are updated. However, Usborne Publishing is not responsible, and does not accept liability, for the content or availability of any website other than its own. We recommend that children are supervised while on the internet.

Hamsters prick up their ears to listen for danger.

Index

Acknowledgements

Cover by Zoe Wray

Photographic manipulation by John Russell, Emma Julings and Zoe Wray

Photo credits

The publishers are grateful to the following for permission to reproduce material:
© **Alamy Images** 13,© **Bruce Coleman** (Alain Compost) 8, (Kim Taylor) 20 and 28; © **CORBIS** (Niall Benvie) cover, (Joe McDonald) 1, (W. Perry Conway) 3, (George McCarthy) 16, (Staffan Widstrand) 19; © **FLPA – Images of Nature** (A. Christiansen) 11, (Foto Natura Stock) 17, (Chris Mattison) 18, (Albert Visage) 21, (Mark Newman) 22; © **Getty Images** (Gary Bell) 5, (JH Pete Carmichael) 9, (Jonathon Gale) 29; © **Heather Angel** (Peter David) 25; **Nature Picture Library** (David Shale) 25; © **NHPA** (Stephen Dalton) 6-7, (Christophe Ratier) 14, (Dr Ivan Polunin) 24; © **Oxford Scientific Films** (Alan Root/SAL) 10, (Doug Bertran/SAL) 15; © **Science Photo Library** (Gregory Dimijian) 23; © **Warren Photographic** (Jane Burton) 27. Photograph on page 31 by Tim Flach.

Every effort has been made to trace and acknowledge ownership of copyright. If any rights have been omitted, the publishers offer to rectify this in any subsequent editions following notification.

Sun, moon and stars

Farm animals

Elizabeth I

RUBBISH AND RECYCLING

Dogs

Horses and ponies

Spiders

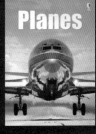
Planes

Ancient Greeks

Cats

VOLCANOES

DINOSAURS

Your Body

Armour

Sharks

Celts

Vikings

Castles

How flowers grow

Digging up the past

Living in space

Caterpillars and Butterflies

Ballet

Pirates

Egyptians

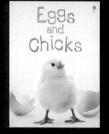
Eggs and Chicks

Romans

Weather

Tadpoles and Frogs

Why do we eat?

Under the sea

Bears

Aztecs

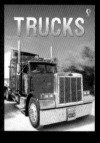
TRUCKS

Night Animals

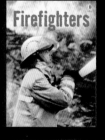
Firefighters

Antarctica

Bugs

COWBOYS

Planet Earth